UC

SCHOOL RESEARCH

AGO

RESEARCH REPORT NOVEMBER 2014

Teacher Evaluation in Practice

Year 2 Teacher and Administrator Perceptions of REACH

Jennie Y. Jiang and Susan E. Sporte

ACKNOWLEDGEMENTS

The authors gratefully acknowledge the Joyce Foundation for its ongoing support as we continue to investigate teacher evaluation in Chicago. We would not be able to build an understanding of the general and specific issues facing the Chicago Public Schools (CPS) as it implements REACH Students without Joyce's long-term commitment.

We would also like to acknowledge the support of CPS and the Chicago Teachers Union (CTU). Our conversations and meetings with Paulette Poncelet, Amanda Smith, and Michael Herring from CPS Central Office and with Carol Caref and Jennifer Johnson of the CTU have informed the content of this report, as have other members of the CPS-CTU Joint Teacher Evaluation Committee.

We thank research assistant Catherine Alvarez-McCurdy for her help in creating endless drafts, and our Steering Committee members for thoughtful comments, especially Arie van der Ploeg, Luis Soria, and Lynne Cherkasky-Davis. As always, colleagues from the University of Chicago Consortium on Chicago School Research have served as readers and thought partners as we conceptualized, analyzed, and wrote up our findings. We especially thank Elaine Allensworth, Jenny Nagaoka, Marisa de la Torre, Holly Hart, Emily Krone, and Bronwyn McDaniel from UChicago CCSR and Alex Seeskin from UChicago Impact for their insightful feedback. Special thanks to Valerie Michelman and Holly Hart for expertise as technical readers and to Jessica Puller for providing a detailed final read. Rachel Levenstein and Stuart Luppescu deserve special recognition for help with survey-related issues.

Finally, and most important, we thank the teachers and administrators of CPS who shared their thoughts through surveys. We know that taking surveys is time consuming, but we could not carry out this work if individual educators and administrators had not put forth this effort. We sincerely hope they see themselves reflected in these pages and we sincerely hope that what they shared can help illuminate the challenges and the opportunities inherent in implementing a complex initiative such as REACH.

We also gratefully acknowledge the Spencer Foundation and the Lewis-Sebring Family Foundation, whose operating grants support the work of UChicago CCSR.

This report was produced by UChicago CCSR's publications and communications staff: Emily Krone, Director for Outreach and Communication; Bronwyn McDaniel, Senior Manager for Outreach and Communication; and Jessica Puller, Communications Specialist.

Graphic Design: Jeff Hall Design
Photography: Cynthia Howe
Editing: Ann Lindner

11.2014/pdf/jh.design@rcn.com

Introduction

In the 2012-13 school year, Chicago Public Schools (CPS) unveiled its new teacher evaluation system, Recognizing Educators Advancing Chicago's Students (REACH Students), in all of its almost 600 schools. Like many districts and states across the nation, Chicago invested considerable resources and energy in overhauling its evaluation system, and there is great optimism these new evaluation systems will improve teacher effectiveness across the district. As the ones being evaluated and the ones conducting the evaluations, teachers and principals[1] are both the primary users and key stakeholders. If teachers and principals are not engaged in the process, these new evaluation systems cannot achieve their goals of improving instructional practices across the district. Teacher and principal perceptions and experiences, therefore, are of great value in understanding the successes and challenges of these new evaluation systems.

As part of our implementation study of REACH, we focus on teacher and principal experiences and perceptions of the new system. In the first year, we found most teachers and principals responded positively. Since then, REACH has continued to evolve; therefore, it is important to gauge whether teacher and principal perceptions have changed. In this brief, we follow up on previous results and share findings on teacher and principal perceptions of the second year of REACH. We look specifically at the degree to which they perceive the system provides fair and accurate measures of teacher effectiveness, and how useful they find it for improving practice.

Across the Nation, Teacher Evaluation Has Changed Rapidly

Within the last five years, the number of states that required annual evaluations for all teachers has nearly doubled, and the number of states requiring the inclusion of measures of student achievement has nearly tripled.[2] The rapid changes in teacher evaluation systems across the country were fueled by both federal Race to the Top funding, which incentivized states to reform their evaluation systems, and an acknowledgement that previous evaluation systems were often unhelpful and ineffective. These previous *"checklist"* evaluation systems provided little information to differentiate teacher performance and often failed to provide actionable feedback and information to teachers.[3] The design of new evaluation systems varies across districts and states, but all attempt to remedy the shortcomings of these previous systems. Most include the components listed in **Table 1**: multiple measures, often including student test score growth;

TABLE 1

New Evaluation Systems are Subtantially Different from Previous Systems

Previous Evaluation Systems	Goals of New Evaluation Systems
Nearly all teachers received high ratings	More differentiation and room for growth
Observations the only measure of performance	Inclusion of multiple measures
"Checklist" tool and vague standards	Use of detailed rubrics defining instruction and providing common language
Untrained evaluators	Extensive training and certification requirements for evaluators
No formal feedback process	Feedback a requirement

1   We use the term "principals" to also include assistant principals, as both can be certified as REACH evaluators in CPS.

2   Rotherham and Mitchel (2014).

3   Weisburg, Sexton, Mulhern, and Keeling (2009).

detailed observation rubrics; trained evaluators; and defined structures to provide feedback to teachers.

CPS was one of the first large urban districts to implement a new teacher evaluation system in all schools. REACH incorporates both a structured observation process and measures of student growth into a teacher's evaluation rating. With over 20,000 teachers, counselors, and staff to be evaluated, unrolling this new system was a massive undertaking, requiring a large-scale investment of time and energy from the district: principals and assistant principals were certified as evaluators, new assessments for non-tested subjects and grades were developed, new data systems to link teachers and students, and to collect and house evaluation results were created, and all teachers, staff, and principals were trained on the new system.

REACH in Its First Two Years

The first year of REACH implementation was well received by both teachers and principals. Overwhelming majorities of teachers reported their evaluators were fair and accurate, found their feedback helpful, and said the observation process supported their professional growth. Principals were also positive; over 80 percent agreed the system was valuable or very valuable both for evaluating teacher performance and for improving instructional practice. However, teachers were concerned about the use of student growth on assessments to evaluate performance, and REACH placed large demands on principal time and capacity.[4]

There were considerable changes in implementation in the second year of REACH. **Figure 1** provides a summarized timeline of some of the key changes, as well as the timing of our surveys. Each of these changes has the potential to modify perceptions of the system. In Year 1, tenured teachers were typically observed only once. These observations did not count, and were intended only to familiarize them with the system. In Year 2, tenured teachers' observations[5] counted toward their REACH rating, potentially impacting their future

Key Elements of REACH

A teacher's REACH rating is comprised of a professional practice score and up to two measures of student growth.

Professional Practice is evaluated through four observations using the CPS Framework for Teaching, a modified version of the Charlotte Danielson Framework for Teaching.

Student Growth Measures

Value-Added: Teachers in tested subjects and/or grades receive an individual value-added score. Most teachers in non-tested subjects and grades receive a school-wide average in literacy value-added score.

Performance Tasks: Performance tasks are written or hands-on assessments designed to measure the progress toward mastery of a particular skill or standard. There are different performance tasks for each subject and grade. Performance tasks are typically administered and scored by teachers.

For more details on REACH measures see Appendix A.

REACH Survey Data

Data for this report are from an annual survey of all teachers and principals:

2014 My Voice, My School (MVMS) Survey
- Administered March 2014
- 19,021 Teachers, 81 percent response rate

2014 UChicago CCSR Principal Survey
- Administered May 2014, 64 percent response rate
- 410 Principals, 378 Assistant Principals

For more details on these surveys, please see Appendix C.

---

4 Sporte, Stevens, Healey, Jiang, and Hart (2013).
5 As required by state law, tenured teachers previously rated Excellent or Superior are on a biennial evaluation schedule. They are observed two times in each of two years and receive

a REACH rating every other year. Tenured teachers previously rated Unsatisfactory or Satisfactory, or missing ratings, were required to be observed four times, and received a REACH rating in 2013-14.

FIGURE 1

REACH Timeline

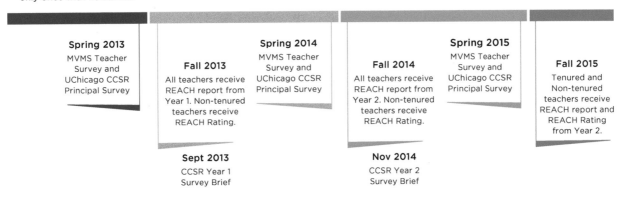

Year 1: 2012-13
Non-tenured teachers, observations begin to count for stakes. Tenured teachers observed only once with no stakes.

Year 2: 2013-14
Tenured teachers' observations begin to count for stakes.

Year 3: 2014-15

Spring 2013
MVMS Teacher Survey and UChicago CCSR Principal Survey

Fall 2013
All teachers receive REACH report from Year 1. Non-tenured teachers receive REACH Rating.

Spring 2014
MVMS Teacher Survey and UChicago CCSR Principal Survey

Fall 2014
All teachers receive REACH report from Year 2. Non-tenured teachers receive REACH Rating.

Spring 2015
MVMS Teacher Survey and UChicago CCSR Principal Survey

Fall 2015
Tenured and Non-tenured teachers receive REACH report and REACH Rating from Year 2.

Sept 2013
CCSR Year 1 Survey Brief

Nov 2014
CCSR Year 2 Survey Brief

Note: Typically, teachers receive tenure in their third or fourth year in the district. All teachers receive REACH reports annually which detail scores on each measure of REACH. Non-tenured teachers receive a summative REACH rating of Unsatisfactory, Developing, Proficient, or Excellent annually. Tenured teachers receive this REACH rating biennially, beginning in Year 2. Tenured teachers missing a prior rating or with prior ratings of Unsatisfactory or Satisfactory were observed four times and received a REACH rating in Year 2. For more details on REACH see Appendix A.

job security. This inclusion of tenured teachers had consequences for principals as well, with the most obvious change being an increase in the number of observations to complete.

Finally, at the time teachers and principals responded to surveys about REACH's first year, they had not received any REACH results. These results were received in September 2013; teachers' knowledge of these results may have influenced their perceptions gathered in spring 2014.

In our ongoing study of REACH, we continue to collect data on teacher and principal perceptions of the new system. These perceptions play a key role in how teachers and principals engage with the new process and support its implementation. In particular, principals need to perceive results to be accurate if they are to utilize them for personnel decisions or to differentiate support. Teachers need to perceive results to be fair and accurate or they will not trust the system and will be unwilling to make changes based on them. In addition, if the system is to inform teacher development, both teachers and principals need to perceive it to be useful for improving instructional practice.

Data for this report were collected from surveys administered in the spring of 2014, before principals and teachers received 2013-14 REACH results. Thus principal and teacher perceptions captured by these surveys may be influenced by their REACH results from the previous school year, 2012-13, which were shared with teachers and principals in the fall of 2013. Below we summarize key findings from our analysis of REACH ratings data from 2012-13.

Under REACH, fewer teachers were rated in the top two categories than in the previous checklist system. Under the previous checklist system, almost all teachers received ratings in the top two categories. In contrast, 2012-13 REACH ratings of non-tenured teachers were concentrated in the middle two categories, and there was an increase in teachers assigned ratings of Unsatisfactory. It is important to note rating category names have changed under REACH and that only non-tenured teachers received final REACH ratings in 2012-13 (see Figure A).

Observation and value-added scores displayed a range of teacher performance. However, almost all teachers received high scores on performance tasks. Observation and value-added scores varied with some teachers scoring at the high end of the scale and some at the low end, while most teachers clustered near the overall average. Performance tasks, however, gave little information on teacher performance, as almost all teachers received high scores.

Observation and individual value-added scores were moderately related. School-wide literacy value-added and performance task scores showed only a weak relationship with observation scores. Observation scores and individual value-added scores are correlated at about 0.3, a moderate relationship that is consistent with relationships measured in other districts. School-wide literacy value-added scores and performance task scores were only weakly related to observation scores with a correlation of about 0.1.

Missing ratings data was a major challenge during the first year of REACH. Twenty-four percent of non-tenured teachers did not receive a REACH rating because they were missing one or more of the four required observations. Teachers with missing REACH ratings default to a rating of Proficient.

Only about 25 percent of all teachers received an individual value-added score. In 2012-13, CPS produced individual value-added scores for teachers who taught reading and math in grades three through eight, accounting for only about a quarter of CPS teachers.[A] Across the district, twice as many elementary teachers are in non-tested subjects or grades as those in tested subjects or grades.

For the full analytic memo visit ccsr.uchicago. edu/teach-eval.

FIGURE A

Fewer Teachers in Top Two Categories under REACH

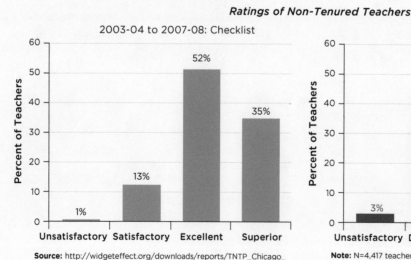

Ratings of Non-Tenured Teachers

2003-04 to 2007-08: Checklist

Source: http://widgeteffect.org/downloads/reports/TNTP_Chicago_Report_Nov09.pdf

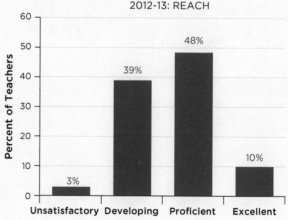

2012-13: REACH

Note: N=4,417 teachers. Graph reflects only non-tenured teachers who received final ratings in 2012-13.

A In 2013-14 the percentage of teachers receiving individual value-added may have increased as high school teachers teaching English, math, science, and/or social studies received value-added scores.

4

Teacher and Principal Perceptions of REACH

Teacher and principal perceptions of the new evaluation system are based on their experiences with each measure of REACH, as well as its implementation. In this second year of REACH, we find that while most teachers and principals remain positive about REACH's potentia—especially the observation process—there is less satisfaction with the overall system; student growth and the time required by REACH continue to be key concerns. Here we share findings from teacher and principal surveys administered in spring 2014 and focus on whether teachers and principals perceive the measures to be fair and whether they feel REACH is useful for strengthening instructional knowledge, skills, and practice. We begin by first discussing how practitioners feel about REACH in general, then focus on perceptions of each measure of REACH, and conclude with teacher and principal concerns about the time and effort REACH requires.[6]

Overall, teachers and principals are optimistic about REACH; however, there is less enthusiasm in Year 2 than there was in Year 1. Most teachers and almost all principals believe in REACH's potential to improve practice. About two-thirds of teachers agreed or strongly agreed when asked if REACH will lead to better instruction and improved student outcomes; and an overwhelming majority (89 percent) of principals agreed or strongly agreed (see Figure 2). However, while the majority of teachers (62 percent) reported being satisfied with the evaluation process at their school, this is a decrease in satisfaction from the first year of REACH, when over 70 percent reported satisfaction with the process (see Figure 3).

Teachers and principals report REACH is changing practice, improving communication, and encouraging collaboration. Teachers reported changing their instruction due to REACH in this second year. Eighty-six percent of teachers agreed or strongly agreed that the observation process has changed their teaching. And over 80 percent of teachers reported changing their teaching to improve their students' scores on performance tasks, NWEA-MAP, or ACT's EXPLORE-PLAN-ACT suite of assessments (EPAS) (see Figure 4). Principals also noted changes in teachers' practice. Over 80 percent said their teachers had changed their instruction to do better on REACH, and almost all reported at least half of their teachers had made noticeable improvements in their classrooms (see Figure 5). Both principals and teachers agreed REACH has improved communication between leadership and staff within their schools. In addition, most teachers reported REACH has improved the quality of their conversations with colleagues, encouraged teachers to collaborate, and influenced their professional development choices.

Beginning teachers are more positive about REACH than teachers with more years of experience.[7] Teachers with five or fewer years of experience in the district are more positive about REACH than those with more years of experience.[8] For example, there was a substantial percentage point difference between beginning and veteran teacher responses to the question of whether REACH will lead to better instruction: 78 percent of beginning teachers agreed or strongly agreed it would, while this was only true for 64 percent of veteran teachers. There was also a systematic difference in overall satisfaction with the system between beginning and

5

---

6   Throughout this section we highlight some of the findings with figures. Others we report in text only.

7   Logistic regression was utilized to ascertain significant differences between groups. See Appendix C for details.

8   Here we define beginning teachers as those with five or fewer years in the district and veteran teachers as those with more than five years. Of survey respondents, 21 percent were beginning teachers and 79 percent were veteran. See Appendix C for details.

FIGURE 2

Most Principals and Teachers Are Optimistic About REACH's Potential to Improve Instruction

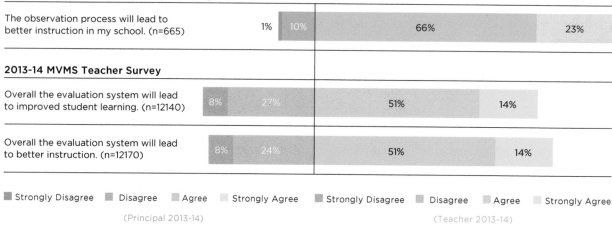

2013-14 UChicago CCSR Principal Survey

The observation process will lead to better instruction in my school. (n=665) — 1% | 10% | 66% | 23%

2013-14 MVMS Teacher Survey

Overall the evaluation system will lead to improved student learning. (n=12140) — 8% | 27% | 51% | 14%

Overall the evaluation system will lead to better instruction. (n=12170) — 8% | 24% | 51% | 14%

■ Strongly Disagree ■ Disagree ■ Agree ■ Strongly Agree   ■ Strongly Disagree ■ Disagree ■ Agree ■ Strongly Agree

(Principal 2013-14)   (Teacher 2013-14)

FIGURE 3

Overall Teacher Satisfaction With the Process Has Declined

Overall, I Am Satisfied With the Teacher Evaluation Process at This School

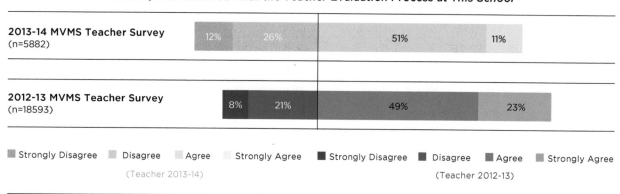

2013-14 MVMS Teacher Survey (n=5882) — 12% | 26% | 51% | 11%

2012-13 MVMS Teacher Survey (n=18593) — 8% | 21% | 49% | 23%

■ Strongly Disagree ■ Disagree ■ Agree ■ Strongly Agree   ■ Strongly Disagree ■ Disagree ■ Agree ■ Strongly Agree

(Teacher 2013-14)   (Teacher 2012-13)

Note: Number of respondents in 2013 and 2014 are significantly different due to randomization of certain questions in 2014. Please see Appendix C for more details. Percentages may not add to 100 due to rounding.

FIGURE 4

Teachers Report REACH Has Influenced Their Teaching

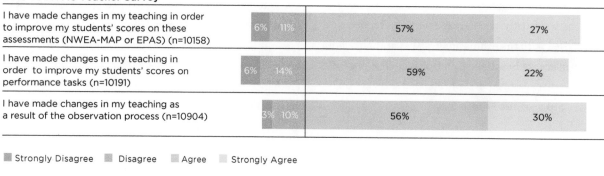

2013-14 MVMS Teacher Survey

I have made changes in my teaching in order to improve my students' scores on these assessments (NWEA-MAP or EPAS) (n=10158) — 6% | 11% | 57% | 27%

I have made changes in my teaching in order to improve my students' scores on performance tasks (n=10191) — 6% | 14% | 59% | 22%

I have made changes in my teaching as a result of the observation process (n=10904) — 3% | 10% | 56% | 30%

■ Strongly Disagree ■ Disagree ■ Agree ■ Strongly Agree

Note: Percentages may not add to 100 due to rounding.

FIGURE 5

Principals Report Most Teachers Have Made Improvements

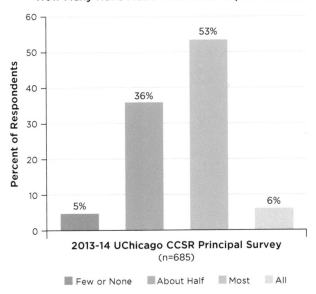

Of the Teachers I've Observed This Year, How Many Have Made Noticeable Improvements?

2013-14 UChicago CCSR Principal Survey
(n=685)

■ Few or None   ■ About Half   ■ Most   ■ All

veteran teachers: 71 percent of beginning teachers said they were satisfied with the system, compared to 58 percent of veteran teachers.

Student Growth: Performance Tasks and Value-Added

Illinois' 2010 Performance Evaluation Reform Act (PERA) requires the inclusion of student growth measures in a teacher's evaluation. In Chicago, student growth is a combination of performance tasks and value-added scores. Performance tasks are district- or school-created assessments administered and graded by teachers. Value-added scores are calculated from either the NWEA-MAP or EPAS. Teachers in tested subjects or grades receive an individual value-added score, and teachers in non-tested subjects and/or grades receive school-wide literacy as their value-added score.[9]

Most teachers believe their evaluation relies too heavily on student growth. In 2012-13 and 2013-14, student growth accounted for up to 25 percent of a teacher's REACH rating.[10] When asked if their evaluation relies too heavily on student growth, 65 percent of teachers agreed or strongly agreed.

Teachers are concerned about the fairness of assessments used to measure student growth; most principals, however, believe student growth can measure teacher effectiveness. Only half of teachers said the assessments used to measure student growth are fair assessments of their students' learning, regardless of whether those assessments are individual value-added, school-wide value-added, or performance tasks (**see Figure 6**).[11] However, most principals (80 percent) agreed or strongly agreed student growth can measure teacher effectiveness.

Special education teachers were especially concerned about the fairness of these assessments. Only about a third of special education teachers said performance tasks or value-added measures were fair assessments of their students' learning. In addition, high school teachers were more likely to disagree with the fairness of the value-added measure than elementary teachers. Sixty-one percent of high school teachers who received a value-added score based on EPAS[12] said it was not a fair assessment of their students' learning, compared to 46 percent of elementary teachers, who received a value-added based on NWEA-MAP.

Professional Practice: Observations

The main element of the REACH evaluation system is the observation process used to rate professional practice, accounting for at least 75 percent of a teacher's REACH rating. The observation process utilizes the CPS Framework for Teaching,[13] a modified version of

7

---

9 See Appendix A for more detail on what comprises a REACH rating and how the percentage of that rating based on student growth has changed between Years 1 and 2.

10 In 2014-15, student growth will account for up to 30 percent of a teacher's REACH rating as required by PERA.

11 All elementary teachers and most high school teachers received student growth scores based on their 2012-13

performance tasks in the fall prior to survey administration; elementary teachers also received 2012-13 individual or school-level value-added scores at that time.

12 High school teachers did not receive a value-added measure in Year 1 of REACH. Year 2 was the first time they received a value-added score.

13 See Appendix B for the CPS Framework for Teaching.

FIGURE 6

About Fifty Percent of Teachers Believe Student Growth Assessments Are Fair Measures

These Measures of Student Achievement Growth Are a Fair Assessment of My Students' Learning

2013-14 MVMS Teacher Survey

Strongly Disagree ■ Disagree ■ Agree ■ Strongly Agree

the Danielson Framework for Teaching. It is structured to provide teachers with information they can use to improve their instructional practices. It includes a pre- and post-conference between teachers and evaluators intended to foster professional conversations and constructive feedback.[14]

Most teachers believe their own evaluators are fair and unbiased. The majority of teachers believe their own evaluator is fair and able to accurately assess their instruction. At least 80 percent of teachers reported their evaluator has at least some level of fairness and accuracy; in fact, over 60 percent said their evaluator is fair and accurate *"to a great extent"* (**see Figure 7**). These results are slightly more positive than they were in Year 1, and are shared by tenured and non-tenured teachers alike. While teachers were generally positive in response to questions about their own evaluator, they still had some reservations about the subjectivity of all evaluators. In fact, when asked about evaluators in general, most teachers (59 percent) agreed the observation ratings depended more on the evaluator than on a teacher's practice.

Most principals believe the observation process is useful in identifying effective teachers and targeting support; however, principals are less enthusiastic in Year 2 than in Year 1. Most principals remain positive about the usefulness of the observation process. Almost 90 percent of principals reported the CPS Framework is useful in identifying effective teachers. About 90 percent reported using observation results to provide targeted support to their teachers; a similar number reported REACH encourages their teachers to reflect on their practice. Seventy percent reported REACH helps them to identify areas on which to focus professional development resources.

While principals remain positive, they are less enthusiastic in Year 2—there were significantly fewer principals who strongly agreed to questions about the Framework's usefulness (**see Figure 8**).

Teachers report the observation process provides useful feedback, encourages reflection, and guides their professional development. Almost 90 percent of teachers said the feedback provided in their conferences included specific suggestions and guidance on how to improve. Furthermore, they said they used the feedback to improve their teaching, and the observation process has encouraged them to reflect on their practice. Almost 80 percent said their observation ratings will influence their future professional development.

---

14 Currently only principals and assistant principals can be certified as REACH evaluators in CPS.

8

FIGURE 7

In Both Year 1 and 2, Most Teachers Believe Their Evaluators Are Fair and Unbiased

2012-13 and 2013-14 MVMS Teacher Survey

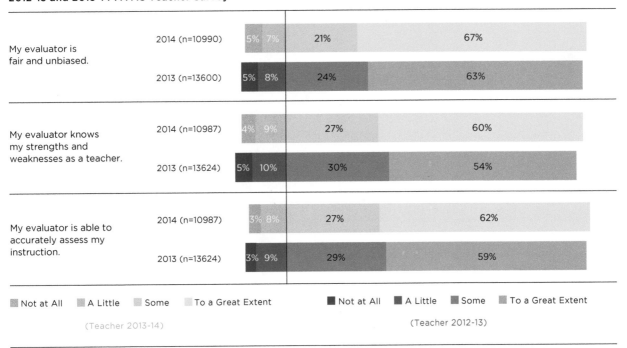

Note: Percentages may not add to 100 due to rounding.

FIGURE 8

In Year 2, Principals Still Positive But Less Enthusiastic About the Framework

2012-13 and 2013-14 UChicago CCSR Principal Survey

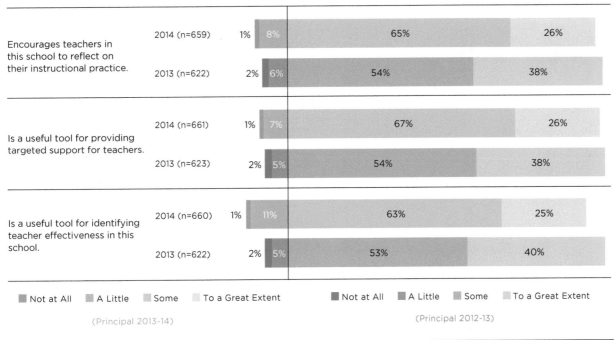

Note: Percentages may not add to 100 due to rounding.

Time and Effort

In Year 1 principals reported on how time-intensive the new system was and how they struggled to balance the additional demands it placed on them. These demands increased in Year 2, as tenured teachers entered fully into the system. For teachers, REACH is more time-intensive than the previous checklist system, which required little of them. REACH requires teachers to administer, grade, and upload performance task scores twice each year, and to participate in pre- and post-conferences, in addition to the observation itself. Teachers are also encouraged to complete pre- and post-conference reflection questions, and to collect and summarize evidence of their professional responsibilities.[15]

Teachers and principals report increased levels of teacher stress and question the effort required by REACH. The large majority of teachers (79 percent) reported that the evaluation process had increased their levels of stress and anxiety. A similar proportion of principals agreed teachers felt more stress as a result of the new system. In addition, both teachers and evaluators questioned the effort required by the process, with almost 60 percent of teachers and 45 percent of evaluators agreeing that the evaluation process takes more effort than the results are worth (see Figure 9).

FIGURE 9

Most Teachers and Some Principals Question the Effort REACH Takes

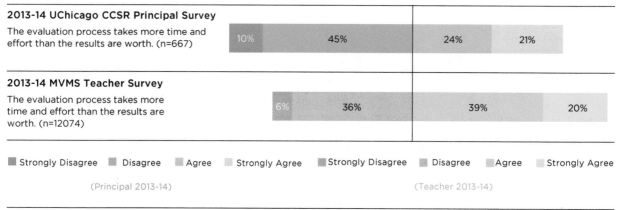

2013-14 UChicago CCSR Principal Survey

The evaluation process takes more time and effort than the results are worth. (n=667)

| 10% | 45% | 24% | 21% |

2013-14 MVMS Teacher Survey

The evaluation process takes more time and effort than the results are worth. (n=12074)

| 6% | 36% | 39% | 20% |

■ Strongly Disagree ■ Disagree ■ Agree Strongly Agree ■ Strongly Disagree ■ Disagree Agree Strongly Agree

(Principal 2013-14)　　　　　　　　　　　　　　　(Teacher 2013-14)

Note: Percentages may not add to 100 due to rounding.

15 Domain 4 of the Framework is Professional Responsibilities and includes professional growth and development, communicating with families, and participating in a professional community.

Summary and Questions to Consider

As survey data from REACH's second year show, participant perceptions about REACH are generally positive, although their responses also identified key concerns. Teachers and principals found the observation process accurate and useful for improving instruction. They agreed the process has potential to improve teaching and learning. Importantly, both teachers and principals reported changes in teacher practice due to observation feedback and student growth results. However, teachers also reported feeling more stress and anxiety, and only half of teachers believed the assessments used to measure student growth are fair; the proportion of special education and high school teachers with concerns about these assessments is even higher. Overall satisfaction with the process has declined, and a majority of teachers and a large minority of principals believed the results were not worth the effort.

These mixed perceptions of REACH are an indication of the complexity of the new system. As REACH enters its third year, these survey responses raise some questions for consideration:

1. How can teachers' concerns about student growth be addressed? Teachers' responses to questions about the student growth part of REACH reveal different, but possibly related, areas of concern. First, a majority of teachers reported their evaluation relies too heavily on student growth. In addition, teachers questioned the assessments themselves. About half of teachers surveyed did not believe any of the student growth assessments used in REACH was a fair representation of their students' learning.

These concerns likely stem from multiple causes. First, scholars continue to debate the usefulness of value-added

measures.[16] The discussion in the popular press remains divided, and teacher evaluation was one of several contentious points in Chicago's 2012 teacher strike. All of this may inform teachers' perceptions. Second, there is no national consensus about how best to include value-added scores for teachers in non-tested grades and subjects. Currently, CPS continues to use school-wide literacy value-added scores for teachers in non-tested subjects and grades, but this practice has been questioned in other states and districts.[17] Third, there continues to be debate in the literature about the degree to which assessments utilizied in value-added measures can detect differences in instruction received by students.[18] Adding to this debate, assessments continue to change. For example, using EPAS to calculate value-added has not been done previously, and soon CPS will move to Common Core-aligned standardized assessments.[19]

Finally, teachers' concerns with the student growth measures may also be rooted in both the complexity of the computation of the value-added scores and how these scores are incorporated in a teacher's evaluation. Value-added scores are derived from statistical models that can be difficult to communicate. Furthermore, the ways different student growth measures are combined vary across teachers; these differences may lead to confusion and concerns about the system's overall fairness. Kindergarten through second grade teachers receive two performance task scores; elementary teachers receive both a performance task and value-added score based on NWEA-MAP; high school teachers receive a performance task rating and value-added score based on EPAS; teachers in tested subjects and/or grades receive an individual value-added score while those in non-tested subject/grades receive a school-wide literacy value-added score.

---

16 For examples, see: Chetty, Friedman, and Rockoff (2011); Glazerman, Loeb, Goldhaber, Staiger, Raudenbush, and Whitehurst. (2010); Kane, McCaffrey, Miller, and Staiger (2013); Rothstein (2010).

17 Baker et al. (2010); Postal (2013).

18 Popham (2007); Polikoff (2010).

19 The Partnership for Assessment of Readiness for College and Careers (PARCC) is the new state assessment and accountability measure for Illinois students enrolled in a public school district. PARCC assesses the new Illinois Learning Standards incorporating the Common Core.

However, teachers' perceptions about how student growth is assessed and calculated could ultimately harm their perceptions of the entire system. Addressing teacher concerns about these assessments and providing transparent, comprehensible information may help; however, the complexity of student growth measures is an issue districts and states will continue to grapple with as teacher evaluation evolves.

2. Can the implementation burden and time demands be reduced without losing the system's usefulness as an agent for change? REACH is undoubtedly time-intensive. Each formal observation requires that both principals and teachers spend time scheduling, preparing for, and participating in a pre-observation conference, observing or being observed, and preparing for and participating in a post-observation conference. Principals must then enter results into the system; teachers are encouraged to answer reflection questions as part of both pre- and post-observation conferences and collect evidence of their professional responsibilities.

That said, these multiple and detailed observations, and teachers' reflections about all facets of their work, are at the heart of instructional change. Instruction is indeed a complex process, and it takes time from both evaluators and teachers to adequately focus on it and to have productive professional conversations about how to make improvements. Furthermore, reducing the number of observations may be counter-productive to the goal of having accurate, fair, and believable ratings. But the whole process wrapped around the evaluation cycle—from scheduling to post-observation conference—makes it complicated to implement for all participants. As REACH enters its third year, it is important to consider how some of the implementation processes might be streamlined in ways that allow more flexibility without reducing the reliability of observation results.

3. How can teachers' levels of stress and anxiety be reduced? There are certainly multiple issues underlying teachers' anxieties about REACH, from concern over their final rating, to the time demands discussed above, to fear that they will be unfairly judged. In addition, the very nature of the instructional process means it will take time for any positive outcomes to be apparent—whether those are sustainable improvements in teacher practice or changes in student outcomes—and teachers may feel it will be difficult to demonstrate improvement. Some of these issues are inherent in any evaluation process in any profession, and will take time, familiarity, and trust between evaluator and teacher to overcome. But the timely and transparent sharing of information may reduce anxiety. In CPS, as in many districts and states, evaluation results have not been provided until the fall—about four months after the school year has ended—typically due to scoring and reporting complexities. This lengthy turnaround time may reduce the relevancy of evaluation results which could potentially undermine the goals of the system.

As Year 2 survey responses show, the majority of participants are optimistic about the system's potential to improve outcomes. But the percentage reporting satisfaction with the system has declined, which may point to a potential trend that could affect the evaluation system's usefulness for its key stakeholders.

This brief and our previous report described participants' perceptions of REACH and its implementation. In the next report in the series, we will explore the ratings themselves. We will describe the results of the observations, performance tasks, value-added scores, and the overall ratings. We will describe the relationship between the different elements of REACH, and look at reliability—the degree to which REACH measures true differences in teacher performance. To the degree possible, we will note any changes between Year 1 and Year 2. We will also take an initial look at teachers' movement across schools and out of the district. Taken together, the perceptions and the analytic data will help paint a more complete picture of Chicago's new teacher evaluation system.

References

Baker, E.L., Barton, P.E., Darling-Hammond, L., Haertel, E., Ladd, H.F., Linn, R.,L., and Shepard, L.A. (2010). *Problems with the use of student test scores to evaluate teachers* (EPI Briefing Paper No. 278). Washington, DC: Economic Policy Institute.

Chetty, R., Friedman, J.N., and Rockoff, J.E. (2011). *The long-term impact of teachers: Teacher value-added and student outcomes in adulthood* (Working Paper No. 17699). Washington, DC: National Bureau of Economic Research Retrieved from http://www.nber.org/papers/w17699

Glazerman, S., Loeb, S., Goldhaber, D., Staiger, D., Raudenbush, S., and Whitehurst, G. (2010). *Evaluating teachers: The important role of value-added.* Washington DC: The Brookings Institution.

Kane, T.J., McCaffrey, D.F., Miller, T., and Staiger, D.O. (2013). *Have we identified effective teachers? Validating measures of effective teaching using random assignment.* MET Project Research Paper. Seattle, WA: Bill & Melinda Gates Foundation.

Polikoff, M.S. (2010). Instructional sensitivity as a psychometric property of assessments. *Educational Measurement: Issues and Practice, 29*(4), 3-14.

Popham, J.W. (2007). Instructional insensitivity of tests: Accountability's dire drawback. *Phi Delta Kappan, 89*(2), 146-155.

Postal, L. (2013). Teachers union suit: Florida's merit-pay law violates U.S. Constitution. *Orlando Sentinel.* Retrieved from http://articles.orlandosentinel.com/2013-04-16/features/os-teacher-evaluations-union-challenge-20130416_1_teachers-union-suit-evaluation-system-test-score-data

Rotherham, A.J., and Mitchel, A.L. (2014). *Genuine progress, greater challenges: A decade of teacher effectiveness reforms.* Boston, MA: Bellwether Education Partners. Retrieved from http://bellwethereducation.org/publication/genuine-progress-greater-challenges

Rothstein, J. (2010). Teacher quality in educational production: Tracking, decay, and student achievement. *The Quarterly Journal of Economics, 125*(1), 175-214.

Sporte, S., Stevens, W.D., Healey, K., Jiang, J., and Hart, H. (2013). *Teacher evaluation in practice: Implementing Chicago's REACH Students.* Chicago, IL: University of Chicago Consortium on Chicago School Research.

Weisburg, D., Sexton, S., Mulhern, J., and Keeling, D. (2009). *The widget effect: Our national failure to acknowledge and act on differences in teacher effectiveness.* New York City, NY: The New Teacher Project.

13

Appendix A
2013-14 Reach Scores And Ratings

A teacher's REACH score is comprised of a professional practice score and up to two measures of student growth. For more details on REACH, visit http://www.cps.edu/reachstudents.

Professional Practice

Teachers are evaluated over multiple classroom observations using the CPS Framework for Teaching, a modified version of the Charlotte Danielson Framework for Teaching (see Appendix B for Framework). Formal observations last at least 45 minutes and include pre- and post-observation conferences. Currently in CPS, only principals and assistant principals can be certified evaluators. To be assigned a REACH rating, a teacher must be observed four times. Non-tenured teachers[20] and tenured teachers with previous low ratings[21] are observed four times annually and receive a REACH rating each year. Tenured teachers with previous high ratings are observed four times over the course of two years and receive a REACH rating every two years, since under Illinois law tenured teachers are evaluated every two years.

Student Growth Measures

To meet Illinois state law requirements about which assessments must be used for teacher evaluation, CPS has identified two different types of student assessments.

Value-Added

Teachers who teach grades 3-8 reading and/or math receive an individual value-added score based on their

students' NWEA MAP—an adaptive, computer-based test. For high school teachers in core subjects, CPS started using the EPAS suite of tests (EXPLORE, PLAN, and ACT) in the 2013-14 school year. Teachers in non-tested subjects and/or grades receive a school-level literacy value-added score.

Performance Tasks

Developed by teams of CPS teachers, individual schools, and/or central office staff, performance tasks are written or hands-on assessments designed to measure the mastery or progress toward mastery of a particular skill or standard. Performance tasks are typically administered and scored by teachers. There are different performance tasks for each subject and grade.

Reach Scores and Ratings

Professional practice scores are combined with student growth scores for an overall REACH score, which ranges from 100 to 400 and translates to a REACH rating of Unsatisfactory, Developing, Proficient, or Excellent (see Table A.1). The percentages of professional practice and student growth are detailed in Table A.2.

TABLE A.1

REACH Ratings and Scores

REACH Score	Rating
100 - 209	Unsatisfactory
210 - 284	Developing
285 - 339	Proficient
340 - 400	Excellent

15

---

20 Teachers in CPS typically attain tenure in their fourth year in the district.

21 Tenured teachers with previous low ratings include those who received an Unsatisfactory or Satisfactory rating on the previous system. Tenured teachers missing previous ratings were to receive four observations and a REACH rating in 2013-14 and then be placed on a biennial cycle in the following year.

REACH Measures

Teachers	Professional Practice (Observations)	Student Growth	
		Performance tasks	Value-added
Elementary educators who teach grade 3–8 English, reading, and/or math	75%	10%	15% Individual
Elementary Pre-K–grade 2 educators	75%	25%	
Elementary grade 3-8 educators who teach non-tested subjects such as science, social science, fine/performing arts, physical education, technology. This category includes librarians	75%	15%	10% School-Wide
High school educators who teach English, math, science and/or social science	75%	20%	5% Individual
High school educators who do not teach English, math, science and/or social science	75%	20%	5% School-Wide
Counselors, related service providers (RSP), educational support specialists (ESS)	100%		

Note: Percentages of student growth for high school educators are different than what was known to educators in the 2013-14 school year. Originally student growth for high school educators who teach English, math, science, and/or social science was 15 percent individual value-added scores and 10 percent performance task scores. For high school educators who did not teach English, math, science, and/or social science, it was originally to be 10 percent school-wide literacy value-added and 15 percent performance tasks. These percentages were updated in the summer of 2014 to reflect the percentages in the table. In Year 3 (SY2014-15) student growth will increase to 30 percent (the minimum required by the State). A student survey may be included, pending the recommendation of the Joint CPS-CTU Teacher Evaluation Committee.

Source: REACH Educator Evaluation Handbook.

Appendix B
The CPS Framework for Teaching

The CPS Framework for Teaching

Adapted from the *Danielson Framework for Teaching* and Approved by Charlotte Danielson

Domain 1: Planning and Preparation

a. Demonstrating Knowledge of Content and Pedagogy
Knowledge of Content Standards Within and Across Grade Levels
Knowledge of Disciplinary Literacy
Knowledge of Prerequisite Relationships
Knowledge of Content-Related Pedagogy

b. Demonstrating Knowledge of Students
Knowledge of Child and Adolescent Development
Knowledge of the Learning Process
Knowledge of Students' Skills, Knowledge, and Language Proficiency
Knowledge of Students' Interests and Cultural Heritage
Knowledge of Students' Special Needs and Appropriate
   Accommodations/Modifications

c. Selecting Instructional Outcomes
Sequence and Alignment
Clarity
Balance

d. Designing Coherent Instruction
Unit/Lesson Design that Incorporates Knowledge of Students and
   Student Needs
Unit/Lesson Alignment of Standards-Based Objectives, Assessments,
   and Learning Tasks
Use of a Variety of Complex Texts, Materials and Resources, including
   Technology
Instructional Groups
Access for Diverse Learners

e. Designing Student Assessment
Congruence with Standards-Based Learning Objectives
Levels of Performance and Standards
Design of Formative Assessments
Use for Planning

Domain 2: The Classroom Environment

a. Creating an Environment of Respect and Rapport
Teacher Interaction with Students, including both Words and Actions
Student Interactions with One Another, including both Words and
   Actions

b. Establishing a Culture for Learning
Importance of Learning
Expectations for Learning and Achievement
Student Ownership of Learning

c. Managing Classroom Procedures
Management of Instructional Groups
Management of Transitions
Management of Materials and Supplies
Performance of Non-Instructional Duties
Direction of Volunteers and Paraprofessionals

d. Managing Student Behavior
Expectations and Norms
Monitoring of Student Behavior
Fostering Positive Student Behavior
Response to Student Behavior

Domain 4: Professional Responsibilities

a. Reflecting on Teaching and Learning
Effectiveness
Use in Future Teaching

b. Maintaining Accurate Records
Student Completion of Assignments
Student Progress in Learning
Non-Instructional Records

c. Communicating with Families
Information and Updates about Grade Level Expectations and Student
   Progress
Engagement of Families and Guardians as Partners in the Instructional
   Program
Response to Families
Cultural Appropriateness

d. Growing and Developing Professionally
Enhancement of Content Knowledge and Pedagogical Skill
Collaboration and Professional Inquiry to Advance Student Learning
Participation in School Leadership Team and/or Teacher Teams
Incorporation of Feedback

e. Demonstrating Professionalism
Integrity and Ethical Conduct
Commitment to College and Career Readiness
Advocacy
Decision-Making
Compliance with School and District Regulations

Domain 3: Instruction

a. Communicating with Students
Standards-Based Learning Objectives
Directions for Activities
Content Delivery and Clarity
Use of Oral and Written Language

b. Using Questioning and Discussion Techniques
Use of Low- and High-Level Questioning
Discussion Techniques
Student Participation and Explanation of Thinking

c. Engaging Students in Learning
Standards-Based Objectives and Task Complexity
Access to Suitable and Engaging Texts
Structure, Pacing and Grouping

d. Using Assessment in Instruction
Assessment Performance Levels
Monitoring of Student Learning with Checks for Understanding
Student Self-Assessment and Monitoring of Progress

e. Demonstrating Flexibility and Responsiveness
Lesson Adjustment
Response to Student Needs
Persistence
Intervention and Enrichment

2012

Appendix C
Data and Analysis

DATA

Data from this brief include surveys of teachers and principals in CPS. Teachers and principals in charter schools were not asked REACH-related items. For more information on the survey, including questions that were asked, see ccsr.uchicago.edu/surveys/documentation.

CPS' My Voice, My School Teacher (MVMS) Survey

This web-based survey was conducted by UChicago Impact in collaboration with Chicago Public Schools and the Illinois State Board of Education. It was administered in March through April of 2014 to all teachers in all CPS neighborhood, charter, selective enrollment, and alternative schools (see Table C.1 for a breakdown of the respondents). In 670 schools, 23,526 classroom teachers were eligible to participate; 19,021 responded (response rate=81%). Survey questions on the teacher survey included questions on leadership, school climate, and teacher collaboration, as well as REACH-related questions.

TABLE C.1

Respondents

	Number of Respondents	Percentage of Respondents
Veteran Teachers (>5 years)	12,661	79%
Beginning Teachers (1-5 years)	3,342	21%
Special Education Teacher	2,450	15%
Classroom Teacher	12,051	75%
Other (counselor, librarian, specialist, etc.)	1,502	9%
High School	4,325	27%
Elementary	11,678	73%

Responses on the MVMS teacher survey are anonymous; we relied on questions within the survey asking respondents their tenure status, subject/grade taught, and years of experience. We used these self-reported indicators to define tenured, special education, and beginning/veteran teacher. Charter teachers were not asked REACH-related questions, as charter schools in CPS do not participate in REACH. Total number of respondents to REACH-related items was 16,003, although the number of respondents varied with each question. In an effort to reduce the length of teacher time spent on the survey, some REACH-related survey questions were randomized; that is, some teachers were randomly selected to answer one group of REACH items and other teachers were randomly selected to answer a different group of REACH items. We tested for differences between the randomly assigned groups and found no significant differences.

UChicago CCSR Principal Survey

We included REACH-related content on UChicago CCSR's annual principal survey. This web-based survey was administered to all principals and assistant principals in May 2014 and had a response rate of 64 percent. In 670 schools, 661 principals were eligible to participate; nine schools did not have a permanent or interim principal during administration. Of the 661 principals, 410 participated (a response rate of 62 percent). In addition, 577 assistant principals from 474 schools were eligible to participate. Of those, 378 participated (a response rate of 66 percent).

Analysis

To test for significant differences between groups, we used logistic regression. Beginning and veteran teachers were defined by responses to the question, *"How many years have you been a teacher* (at CPS or somewhere else)*?"* Teachers who responded five years or fewer were considered beginning teachers and teachers who responded more than five years were considered veteran teachers (analysis on more fine-grained years of experience [first years, 1-2 years, 3-5, 6-10, 11-15 and more than 15] was also conducted). Special education teachers were defined as teachers who selected *"Special Education Teacher"* from a question asking teachers their teaching position. *"Other"* was defined as respondents who selected *"Other* (counselor, librarian, specialist, etc.)*"*; however, there were not enough respondents in the category to discern differences.

Our models used binary outcomes based on the response categories, comparing those who answered in the two top response categories (strongly agree or agree) against those who answered in the bottom two response categories (disagree or strongly disagree).

For example, to compare responses of beginning and veteran teachers, we utilize the following model:

$$logit \, [\, p(x_i)] = \beta_0 + \beta_1 \, beginningteacher_i$$

where p = the probability the response is strongly agree or agree; i = respondent

To compare high school teacher responses and elementary teacher responses and to compare special education teacher and non-special education teacher responses we controlled for tenure status as well:

$$logit \, [\, p(x_i)] = \beta_0 + \beta_1 \, spedteacher_i + \beta_2 tenure_i$$

where p = the probability the response is strongly agree or agree; i = respondent

The odds ratios shown in **Table C.2** support the findings on differences between groups. If the odds ratio is close to or equal to 1, then there are no significant differences between groups. Odds ratios significantly greater than 1 indicate the particular group is more likely to agree or strongly agree; those significantly less than 1 indicate a particular group is less likely to agree. **Table C.2** shows differences between beginning and veteran teachers. For example, beginning teachers were significantly more likely to agree or strongly agree that they had made changes in their teaching as a result of the observation process, as indicated by the odds ratio being significantly above 1 (odds ratio=2.727).

TABLE C.2

Beginning Teachers/Veteran Teachers

	Odds Ratio	Std Error
The observation rubric is a fair representation of good teaching	1.741**	-0.087
My observation ratings will guide my future PD choices	1.761**	-0.099
My evaluation results will strongly influence my future PD activities	1.548**	-0.079
I have made changes in my teaching as a result of the observation process	2.727**	-0.215
The evaluation process has increased my level of stress and anxiety	0.958	-0.068
My evaluation relies too heavily on Student Growth	0.519**	-0.031
Overall, I am satisfied with the teacher evaluation process at this school	1.798**	-0.114
Overall, the evaluation system will lead to better instruction	1.987**	-0.095
Overall the evaluation system will lead to improved student learning	1.724**	-0.078

Note: Asterisks indicate a significant effect: ***p<.01, **p<.05, *p<.10. The excluded group in this example is veteran teachers.

ABOUT THE AUTHORS

JENNIE Y. JIANG is a Research Analyst at UChicago CCSR. She is currently working on an evaluation of the Urban Teacher Education Program (UChicago UTEP), in addition to her work on teacher evaluation. Previously, she was a teacher in both Chicago Public Schools and in Shenzhen, China. She earned an MPP in public policy at the University of Chicago and an MS in education at Northwestern University. Jiang's research interests include teacher preparation, quality and support, school leadership, and school choice.

SUSAN SPORTE is Director for of Research Operations at UChicago CCSR. Her current research focuses on teacher preparation, measuring effective teaching, and schools as organizations. She serves as main point of contact with Chicago Public Schools regarding data sharing and research priorities; she also oversees UChicago CCSR's data archive. Sporte received a BS in mathematics from Michigan State University, an MA in mathematics from the University of Illinois at Springfield, and an EdM and EdD in administration, planning, and social policy from the Harvard Graduate School of Education.

CPSIA information can be obtained
at www.ICGtesting.com
Printed in the USA
LVHW071056230723
753216LV00002B/63